EARLY TO MID-INTERMEDIATE

Soaring on Air

THREE PIANO SOLOS BY
NAOKO IKEDA

ISBN 978-1-4234-0734-3

WILLIS MUSIC

EXCLUSIVELY DISTRIBUTED BY

HAL•LEONARD®
CORPORATION
7777 W. BLUEMOUND RD. P.O. BOX 13819 MILWAUKEE, WI 53213

In Australia Contact:
Hal Leonard Australia Pty. Ltd.
4 Lentara Court
Cheltenham, Victoria, 3192 Australia
Email: ausadmin@halleonard.com

Visit Hal Leonard Online at
www.halleonard.com

Soaring on Air

FOREWORD

This collection of pieces has the word "air" in the title. This could literally mean the air, the wind, the sky, the environment—or, it could mean a simple melody. Many Baroque and Classical works have the word "air" in their titles, and I have intentionally used it here so that it will give you both a visual image and a sense of melody as you play these pieces.

The poems that follow are not lyrics to accompany the pieces, but may serve as further guidance to understanding the music. They were very much an inspiration to me.

I hope that these pieces inspire you to open your heart, and to spread your own wings.

Naoko Ikeda

WINGS OF THE RAINBOW
A-flat major 4/4 – Moderato

In the very first measure, two rainbows are drawn in the music! Pay particular attention to the contrasting dynamics throughout this piece. See also if you can find an inverted diminished 7th chord.

I'm soaring through two rainbows,
Splashed in the sky after rain.
My heart flies, too —
It means today,
I will see you.

WINGS OF SAND
G minor 6/8 – Andantino

As you play this poignant melody, imagine tiny grains of sand being carried away by the wind.

Tears drop endlessly,
Swept away by wings of sand.

Rustle, rustle
The dry wind blows.
Rustle, rustle
The tears turn to light!

Someday I will see
the ocean, over the dune.

WINGS OF SNOW
F-sharp minor 4/4 – Andante

The melody to this piece is simpler than the other two; however, in a way it is a much more passionate piece. Reflect on inner change happening, rather than expressing outward emotion. Bring out the left-hand melody whenever it occurs.

Snow falls in my soul,
White and quiet
Like a feather.

My joys and sorrows alternate,
Like the colors of the seasons.
Reborn –
In the muted calm of midnight.

The snow outside is soft and calm.
And my heart is warm, content.

(TRANSLATION OF POEMS BY TAKAKO TERANISHI)

Wings of the Rainbow

Naoko Ikeda

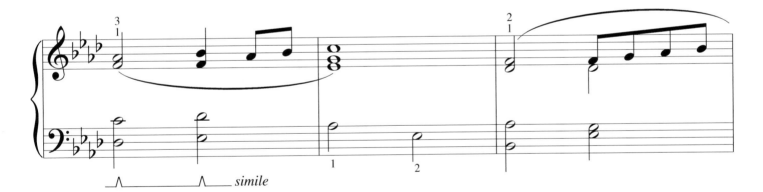

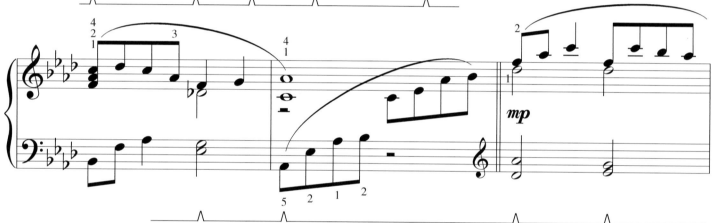

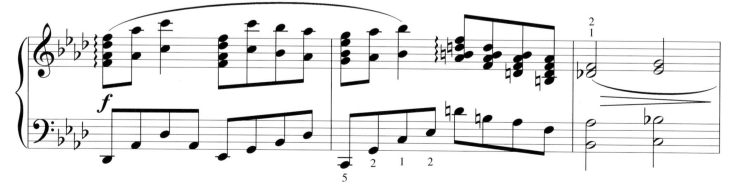

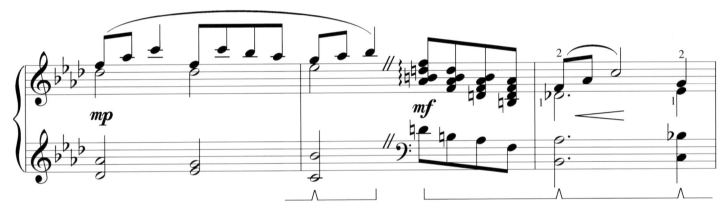

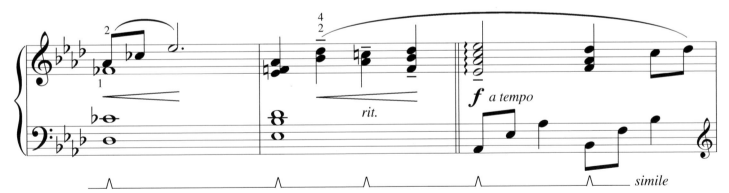

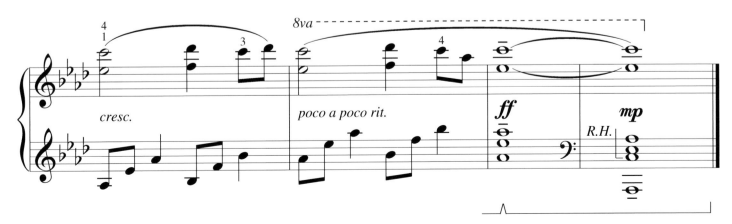

Wings of Sand

for Rieko Ikegaya

Naoko Ikeda

Andantino

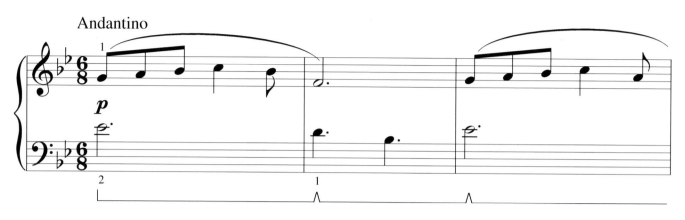

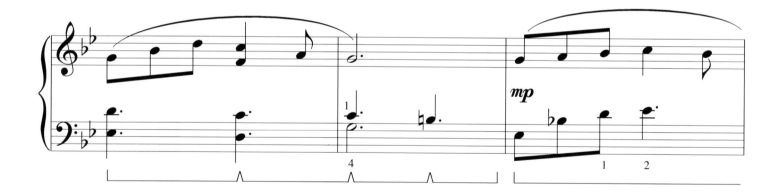

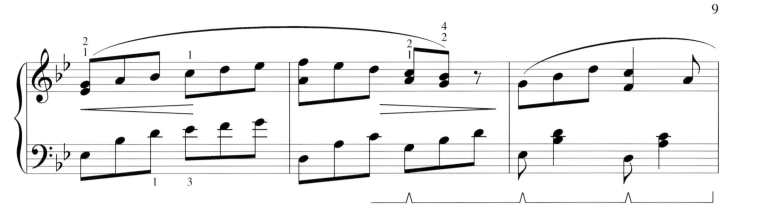

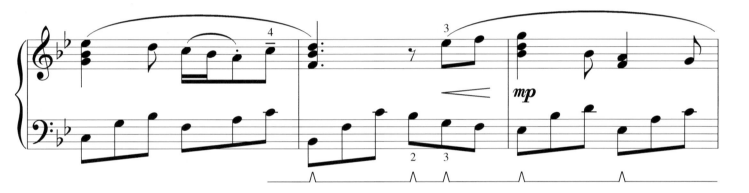

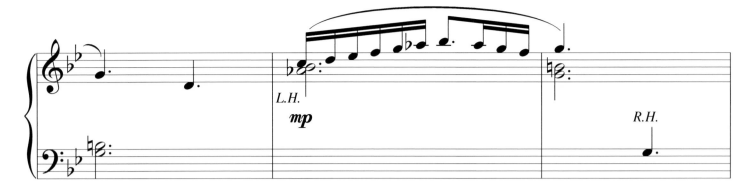

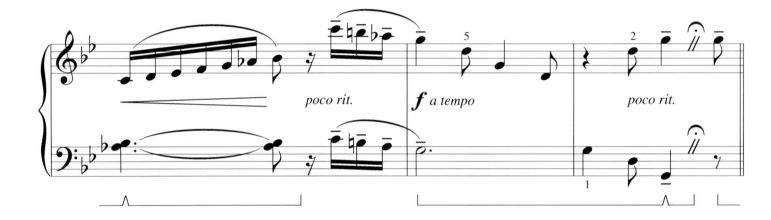

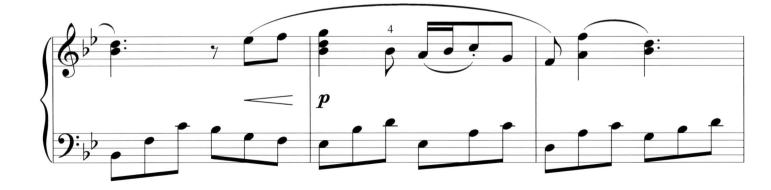

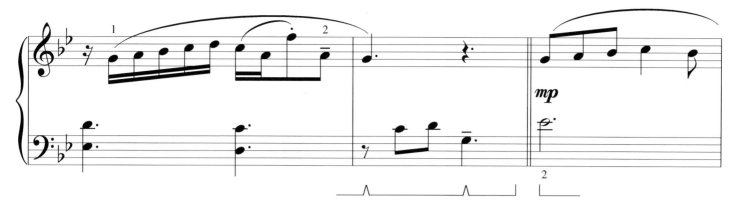

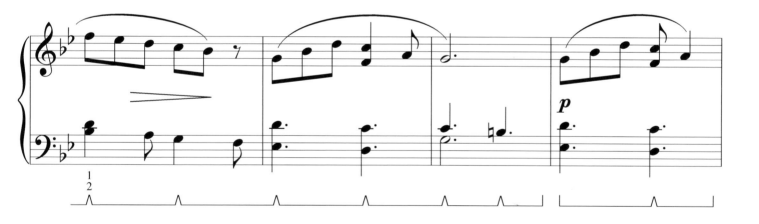

Wings of Snow

for Hiroko Fujimoto

Naoko Ikeda

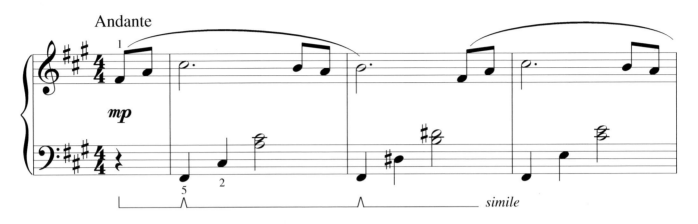

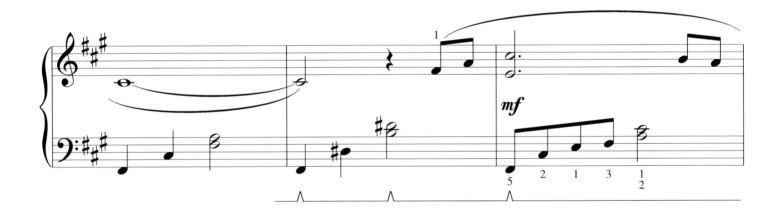

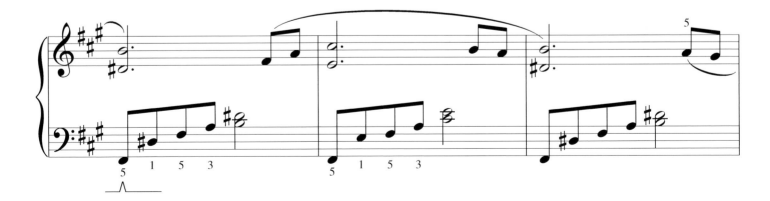

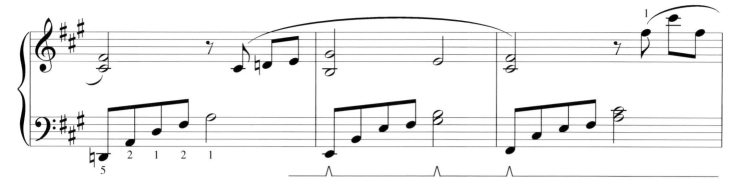

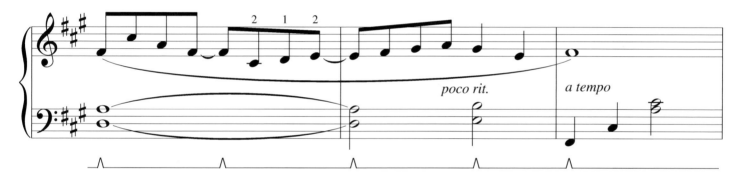

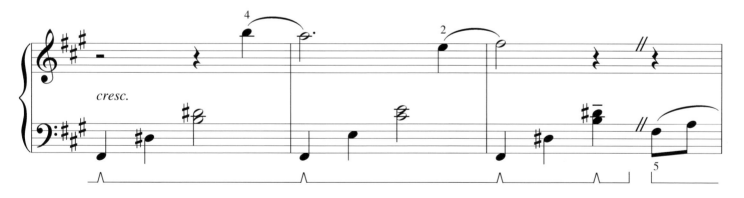

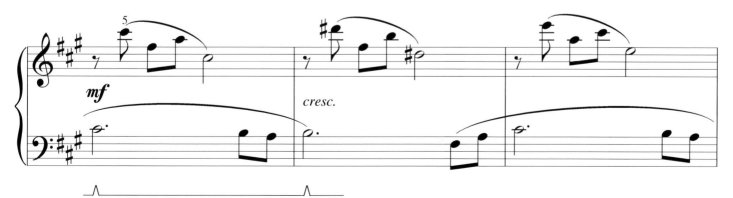

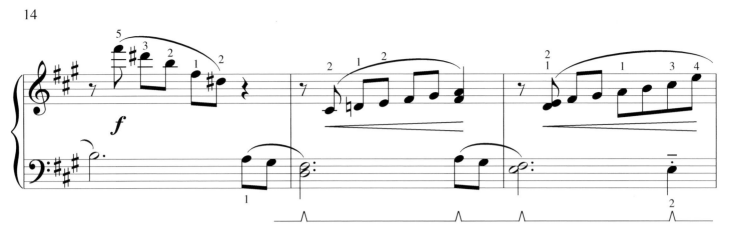

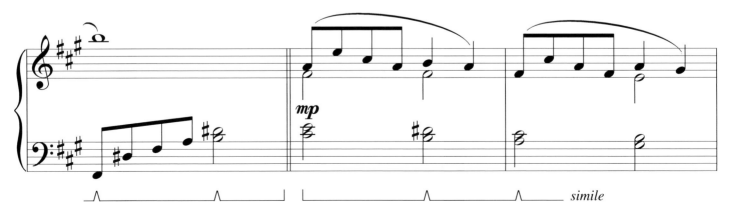

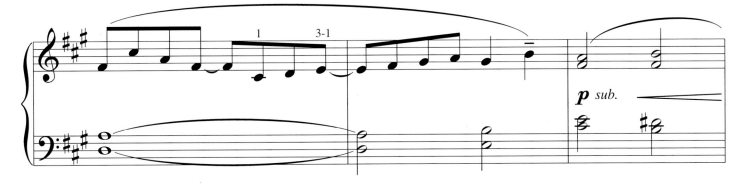

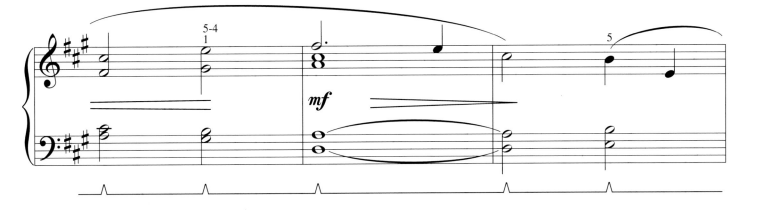

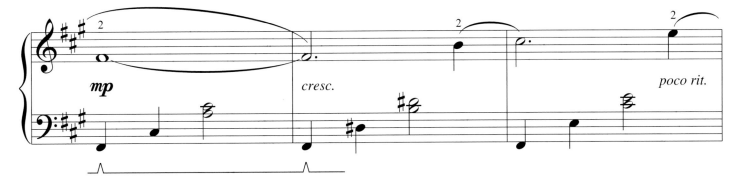

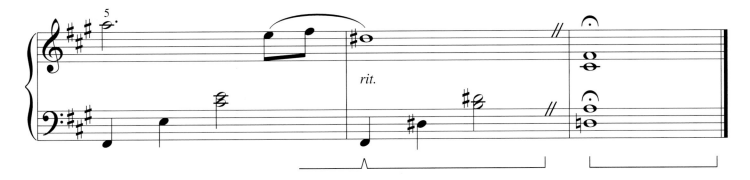